# First Things Last

## Also by David Malouf

**Poetry**

"Interiors" in *Four Poets*
*Bicycle and Other Poems*
*Neighbours in a Thicket*
*Poems 1976-77*
*Wild Lemons*

**Prose**

*Johnno*
*An Imaginary Life*

# First Things Last

## Poems by David Malouf

University of
Queensland Press

Published by University of Queensland Press, St Lucia, Queensland, 1980

© David Malouf, 1980

This book is copyright. Apart from any fair dealing for the purposes of private study, research, criticism, or review, as permitted under the Copyright Act, no part may be reproduced by any process without written permission. Enquiries should be made to the publishers.

Printed and bound by Watson Ferguson & Co., Brisbane

Published with the assistance of the Literature Board of the Australia Council.

*National Library of Australia*
*Cataloguing-in-Publication data*

Malouf, David, 1934-
    First things last.

    ISBN 0 7022 1564 3
    ISBN 0 7022 1565 1 Paperback

    I. Title.

A821'.3

## CONTENTS

Wild Lemons  *1*
The Garden  *2*
The Martyrdom in Room Fourteen  *4*
Preludes  *5*
Elegy: the Absences  *11*
For Two Children: Lelo and Alex Tesei  *15*
Deception Bay  *16*
Reading a View  *24*
*Three Prose Poems*
    The Ladders  *25*
    The Switch  *26*
    Carpenter's Shed  *27*
The Crab Feast  *28*
First Things Last  *38*
Ode One  *41*
A Poor Man's Guide to Southern Tuscany  *44*
An die Musik  *51*
Ode: Schubert, Sonata in B Flat Major, D.960
  (op. posth.)  *53*
Ode: Stravinsky's Grave  *56*

**AUSTRALIAN EMBASSY**
GODESBERGER ALLEE 107
5300 BONN 2

Many of these poems were written with the assistance of a
Fellowship from the Literature Board of the Australia Council.
The author wishes to thank the Board for their generosity and
encouragement.

# WILD LEMONS

*For Don Dunstan*

Through all those years keeping the present
open to the light of just this moment:
that was the path we found, you might call it
a promise, that starting out among blazed trunks
the track would not lead nowhere, that being set
down here among wild lemons, our bodies were
expected at an occasion up ahead
that would not take place without us. One
proof was the tough-skinned fruit among
their thorns; someone had been there before us
and planted these, their sunlight to be sliced
for drinks (they had adapted
in their own way and to other ends); another
was the warmth of our island, sitting still
in its bay, at midnight humming
and rising to its own concerns, but back,
heat-struck, lapped by clean ocean waters
at dawn. The present is always
with us, always open. Though to what, out there
in the dark we are making for as seven o'clock
strikes, the gin goes down and starlings
gather, who can tell? Compacts made
of silence, as a flute tempts out a few
reluctant stars to walk over the water
and a famous beard, benignly condescending,
looks on. I lie down
in different weather now though the same body,
which is where that rough track led. Our sleep
is continuous with the dark, or that portion of it
that is this day's night; the body
tags along as promised to see what goes.
What goes is time, and clouds melting into
tomorrow on our breath, a scent of lemons
run wild in another country, but smelling always of themselves.

## THE GARDEN

In some lights it is simple:
versions of green,
leaf and underleaf, tree
orchids, a fabric of vine

and flower and vine dense woven.
It might be original
as They first saw it — high,
sunless, breathing, a wall

called God, earth-rope and cloud-rope
tangled. And was
there sky? Had they caught its colour
already in butterflies?

They tore the voices
away, silence was blue.
The wall sighed like an arras
and fell. When they stepped through

they were not themselves; far off
seemed closer, they stood
on flat boards in a world
of perspectives, while a cloud

one only, a message pinned
to the ceiling, climbed
out of earshot and was lost.
It must have seemed

the far end of things.
It was in fact a start
in a fresh direction, a green
shoot, a co-ordinate.

As when a songbird sketches
three notes on the air: one
then another at a tangent,
then the first found new again.

# THE MARTYRDOM IN ROOM FOURTEEN

The swordstroke and their arms' weight, double-fisted, carries through,
   away from
the moment. The miraculous decollation severs
trunk from head as grassblades
shiver, the spirit soars, body pitches
back into local weather. So a saint
is bundled through the gates of Paradise, and the hired agents
of this world in their naked sweat and muscle, having fulfilled
the contract, are recalled
to the body's business: one heel
raised to take the blow, they swing away in the acceptance
of gravity, the sadness of the flesh. Behind them
crumbling hill towns move into the distance
of evening, drawn by oxen
clouds of dust roll in over the fields. Tensed
here for the connoisseur's appraising eye, the executioners
of light, paid to deliver the *coup de grâce*
in an elegant ecstatic dance are still
stained and sweaty with it, the shock of blood. They take our breath
with their brute and sudden beauty. Our heads
are stunningly struck off, go rolling into
the stickiness of grass, wet green, as stroke on stroke it thunders
about us. The event
like a good joke catapults
our head into one dimension, our body into
another, but most of all it fills the gap with solid blue where all things
   are
connected. A common landscape takes the sun
and reassembles it in seven colours, each a sense.
The workmen stoop, resume
their gear; feeling the tug of
a world over their shoulder, where there is other work to do before
winter — a harvest to be got in.

# PRELUDES

*For Bruce and Brenda Beaver*

I

Today: we have come through it
and beyond. It is almost
tomorrow. We have arrived at the near edge
of a stubble field that shelves toward bluer weather.
At the far end it is pinewood
then air. In some other quarter of the sky they say
it's foggy; there are warnings to small shipping
of gales et cetera; but here as far
as the eye can see it's full
summer, a fair beginning, and we
are making without haste across the scene; light sizzles
on our shoulder-blades, we flush up
crickets that climb my trouser-legs and leap, a minor grace,
from my shirtfront, perform
in your hair. Another couple,
and a child who was alone collecting pebbles, have gone off left
by a downward path that leads — can't you smell it?—
to surf; we do not miss them. First
the small grass and its creatures, later pines.
Then, at the end of this field
another; or a parcel of the same that after
forest and grass from this side has the look of
(in one of its many moods) a stretch of air.


II

The road climbs uphill into
the sun. It is
earth worn flat
with footsteps. Blossoms

nod above the light that has been
beaten up (such heavy
traffic!) and the bees
work along it. Forests

of a cloudlike blue begin
on either side, they roll to
horizons. It would depend
on how you see it whether

this path leads to the world
or back from it; earth
does not run to distinctions.
Sometimes I am on

the road, sometimes
my shadow is and I
am not. It makes no odds.
Bees fossick gold

where they find it, transmuting
dust into clouds
of froth-pale future forests
that dream in the boughs

of this one. Another
road must run
between. I follow it.
At home wherever I am.


III

Dawn flares along the edge of an office block: knife
-like unseals an envelope
the new day delivers.

This section of the grid
works with the muddled cries, the uneasy cornering
of a bad dream's used-car salesyard and a river
sliding into dawn, the scattered debris
of the night sky still upon it. All we were given
and had, and then pretended not to hear,
fills the street with traffic, desperate
souls stamping for out through a long cool drink that might be gin,
a blue spell between showers or a blond head turning
away in wisps of windblown cloud that leaves us
trampolining high out of the smog
but leaves us just the same and who is happy
to be the same or left? The moment hovers:
too simple to be true, an ambiguity turned over
reveals the underside
of freeway happenings. Something is carried
forward beyond all this, that can't be left
on a seat at small bus-stations. A residuum
settles on all things and glows like space dust sifting
towards us; or occasions move
in the opposite direction, space eddies
out of them, they glow from
within.

IV

The world is as if
after rain. Things wear their instant
original sheen

before thumb print
or boot. Roof tiles laid
at a keen diagonal

define a perfect wedge
of air that clouds move into,
a bird flies out of; several

leaves shine. In my head
the tree goes all the way
down, out of sight

at street level touches
the earth. All is
in its fragments set right

in the frame, and washed
are the various grey
and grey-brown city colours.

As if after rain
is a corner of and posits
the whole. But here

such arguments move out
of view, like a bird between
office blocks that makes for,

we guess, some spot of green as if
Eden (or as we
set off, so we assume).


V

The day is open
on all sides. Little clouds
puff out of my head, and a few free
performances divert
the air, so easily dented since it gives
and gives more than we need
of it to feed our bodies with its blue, or
our spirit with what trickles
up, invisible, as things push through out of themselves
to the far side of the picture.

     On that side
too the day is open. A shadow enters;
the rest of course must follow. So we wait, eyes covered
by the hands of one who steps out of the fog
behind us.
     Let the angel
speak before you answer. The first word
that flies into your head,
but *now*, will be the last word of its text.


VI

Expected, it will appear like any other
at the proper hour, inheriting its weather
from last night's stars, a ripple
of frog spawn on the lake's
too lucent foliage, its glassy forest: a morning
quick with departures. Over the flat land the sky
moves mountains of breath. Something new
has crept into the scene, the whole lake shivers. Out of
an evergreen that branches
downward in its depths, a boy, bare-legged, clambers through
towards real grass and makes for the horizon.
I turn, watch his shadow
grow near. The pace of things
quickens, as if the day suddenly found itself translated
to a new nervous system, all its greens
tuned up a pitch, air at a cooler tension
on the surface of the skin. A head
swivels through a hundred and eighty degrees, I see myself
at a distance reappear
as *me*, as in the phrase *someone is watching
me* or beyond the morning's frame of reference
*aims at me*. And a hat I haven't worn since I was a kid
at high school spirals

up, out through a hole between the clouds not much bigger
than a head, taking with it
whatever was under it
once, all those adolescent yearnings
after fame or love or fast cars tearing off down numbered highways.
The landscape goes on breathing
the open air, as huffing, I jog regretfully away after
a hat or some such lost thing. Finding
my way out among clouds, I lift
a tent flap — circus music! and slip in free under the skyline.

## ELEGY: THE ABSENCES

*G.M., 1896-1964*

Tree crickets tap tap tap. They are tunnelling
their way out of the dark; when they break through,
their dry husks will be planets. Little sheep-bells
clink. The sheep are finding their way down
through clouds, and fence by fence into the distance
dogs bark, clearing ditches, marking farms.
Much that is living here goes into the mouth
of night or issues from it. I sleep, and silence
climbs into my ear, the land blacks out, all
that was delicate and sharp subdued with fog.
The dead are buried in us. We dream them
as they dreamed us and woke and found us
flesh. Their bones rise through us. These are your eyes:
you will see a new world through them. This is your tongue
speaking. These are your hands, even in sleep
alert like animals. Stumbling on
down known paths through blackberry canes I happen
on details that insist. They scratch, they drag
their small hooks, they whiplash, they draw blood.

•

You balloon above me, a big cloud burning
with breath; a coolness settles on my skin.
Your hands that could manage
things gone wrong, stopped clocks, a generator
with the devil in it, roughly set me right.

You talk, you stroke my brow, I come back into
the house: clean plates on shelves, the simple view
— a world that's workable.
I'm safe, I'm held. As when you found a greenie's
thin-shelled, sky-pale egg and brought it to me. Look,

you said. I looked. In the round nest of your hand
a landscape, water, stories, even my own
small life. In your palm,
roughened from work, a cat's cradle of lines,
leading to where I was, to where I am.


•


In a century when it was some men's fate to be
marshalled into firing squads, and others'
to go to the wall (the meat-eating

angels of those years snapped through the air
like bullets and left wounds that peace could not
grow over; even those like you who lived

at peace, had also bled); in a century
when wheatcrops passed three times through the same belly
as mud, as mud, a man walked out

of a tale you told and stood knee-deep in ashes
on the moon. Your days so common I can find
no mark of "history". But I see you rub

a sore place on your skull, wondering where
it struck, what day, what hour, and how
you picked the beginnings up of a story we

are seeing, no not the end but say the climax
of. The man goes on out of your mouth and into
silence, hangs on a breath. What happens next?


•

You bore my image long enough, the promise
of it, looking clean through the bodies
of women to where I stood beside the river
waiting, pitching stones. No wonder I stand there
still. No wonder I bear the image of you
to the edge of streams in every weather, looking
back through the bodies
of women, strangers, searching for the one
door I must come through. I look back
through it, beyond the wars: a regatta day;
grass, white lace verandas. You are there. You are looking
towards me. The woman is still, turning neither
your way nor mine, she does not know us.
She will.
    The river is always the same river.
Stones skip light across it. Generations
of fish, wave upon wave, shoulder upstream.

•

You knew about absences. I am learning
slowly how much space they occupy
in any house I move to, any page — the white spaces
no ink flows into, the black ones
no breath flows out of, mouths. My mother lived
for eight years in your absence. Now we make room
for hers. The ghostly bodies we grew out of
are still somewhere within us. We look through them
to what lies ahead. Back behind
is greener than it was for all those deaths.

•

The house catches its breath. I go downstairs
in the dark: stars at the window, a tap drips
cold. I stoop and drink from a cupped hand,
cradling the sweet water. It is more
than water when I lift it to my lips.

A barefoot child on the cool boards of a house
I left decades ago, I pause and hear
your footfall on the landing. *Is that you
son?* I dare not answer. If I went and stood
in the dark well looking up, would you be there?

## FOR TWO CHILDREN:
Lelo and Alex Tesei

Across the lake the small houses appear
to be real, or to imagine themselves somehow
painted on the view and leaning toward
their shaky selves in water, taking the sun
for granted, stretching their timbers, half asleep
in a dream of such apparent permanence
that we hire a boat and would row across to visit,
or walk there if we could, watching fishes
snap their tails beside us and the mirror
scales reflect us tiny on their backs.

Instead we trail our hands under a jetty
and stay close in to shore. The water is clear,
metallic, deep, with an edge so keen our hands
are struck off at the wrist, set in Peru, say,
or Alaska, in a reliquary of solid
rock crystal. No longer ours, they seek
adventures. In the houses opposite, across
the blue-black glassy lake they stroke a cat
or crumble cup-cakes, saying we should have come there
too. And indeed we should, in a hired dinghy

and a swirl of smoke over icy pebbles, trailing
our oars and flicking crumbs of rainbowed sunlight
at fishtails in our wake. But the houses seem
no nearer. At arm's distance our hands give up
a career of pins-and-needles and drift back
to a warm, a known continent. Only the fish
rise to the surface and their round mouths gape.
We lean to where the boat tugs at its shadow
down there, blue-black and deep. Where have you been
all day? they ask at the boatshed on the beach.

## DECEPTION BAY

I

That house is no longer there. Cloud shadows
slide through its walls, a rabbit sniffs
at the threshold: moonlit rubble and a fireplace
smoky with briar roses. When ghostly rain falls in my sleep
I hear, under the sky, a tin roof drumming that is not
the roof over my head. When I pause to read
from cupboard shelves what happened
to us, what happened
without us, floorboards tilt, dull windows take
the sheen of open water.
    That house
is far out at last, moving fast
on its fabulous voyage,
and further beyond events.


II

Out there, beyond the drizzle
of light over the shoals, grey
oyster-shells cling
to piles, moonlit houses
unmoored, slip off into
fog, darkness drops
from the pines. It is night,
is it? that comes on,
or smoke, or forgetting.
Too late a new colour
enlivens the facts
of autumn. When I go
back, turning
a pine cone in my greatcoat
pocket, patches

of dark have grown all over
so much of it, so many
places can't be entered.
There are occasions
here, where midnight
never lets up. Even
the crabman's boy, his eyes
wrinkling, sees nothing
but the shadows that pour from
my lips. He shakes
his head; as in
a room at the back
of my head coaldust settles
on furniture, on faces:
*No. I don't know you.*


III

Four empty chairs, a room
where it rains. I go back
and the chairs now are set
on four sides of a table

that has long since been assumed
as smoke from a woodpile.
The chairs, just settling out
of their cloud, tilt a little,

the four legs not quite grounded
— yes now, as I bring them
down. It's a beginning
in the ashen rain. Lawyer

canes wind through the rounded
cane of their backs.
Later I shall try
for spoons and a soupbowl,

the breath of a grace
will reconstruct itself
as words, mouths,
a family assembled.

Windows meanwhile
are holes where out of
the long rain we come back
singing. At the centre

of the house a room well-lighted;
at the centre
of the room, four chairs
and a trap, a table, set.


IV

The light is afternoon.
Familiar landmarks
have stepped off into
such distance as early
in the century was still
to be met with and left
behind as so much dust
on a faded lithograph. Innocence
we call it, condescending
as so often to our forebears,
whose eyes look too clearly
through us to what lies
ahead. Though what I meant
to speak of and to draw
from the scene was another
unlooked-for destination,

as settling
their wraps about them, touched
with twilight and the glow
of a day's trek through pinewoods, three
in a dinghy push out from
the present. Only their laughter
reaches us. Already where they are going
lays its shadow on them.
*We meant to row*
*to the little limestone cove and now look*
*where we've got to.* I look over
my shoulder, and the sandy
beach is too far off
to be visible, though they
have been there and rowed on.
I look back and laugh
at that glum figure hugging
himself, alone there
at the point where I began
this business, eye
screwed into a spyglass. Stars
come out, sudden sparks
that leap in the dark
over fences. Paddles,
dripping, draw the thin
horizon line towards us.
We are four.


V


We are standing hand in blue hand under
an avalanche of leaves, having wandered off
in the heat of instant thunder into the sea
of sound, the clashing of stones they call Australia

and will not be found. Light settles on the last
of a trail of crumbs; seeds drift and flare; our parents
calling, part the grass. And though we know
already what we are called, we let our names

slip by and do not answer, lost in the game
of being lost, expecting at a hand-clap
to jump through to the real event, a story
more green, more January. Quiet as stones

at the bottom of a stream, we watch its outline
approach and hold our breath. The sun snags, dripping
red, night starts to happen, my sister weeps.
Of mother's moons the lesser, I tell myself,

where she tugs and rides, a polkadot disturbance
at the brink of where I am. The searchers bump
in the dark, then break and stumble, crying *Where
are they? Why don't they answer?* Colours fall

from their clothes, the stars rise through them; they push through
    clouds
into still rooms, doorless, thick with breath, and sigh
and stare. They are years off now and past all calling.
We call and call, tears shine in pools around us.

Far out on banks of light like shifting water
two figures, small, grief-stricken, brave the dark.
*Where are we? Whose dream is this?* They stoop and plunge
their stiff arms elbow-deep in the mirage.


VI

By slow turns I arrive at
    the point of understanding:
I am eight, I go out into
    a blacked-out suburb

of the moon. Other children
   are sleep-walking there, playing
hopscotch on blank pavements.
    Tramtracks run

into dark at the terminus; somewhere beyond
   the seafront, the sea, a brass band
thumping; and all along
   the street front doors

stand open (such innocence)
   to whatever might break in.
A collective cry goes up and we fall
   still as it draws

its long breath over us. In house
   after house at the same moment
the same event: a woman's
   hand in sleep goes out

to the empty place in the double bed, her mouth
   fills with a sound of
lamenting. All night-games there
   break off. A single shadow

sways over our heads, dropping
   dead leaves into
the hands of all those women:
   a tree of telegrams.


VII

Over the bay quicksilver
mornings hang still
on the postman's whistle bringing

rain squalls, foreign postmarks,
ill news
of the capitals that sink

towards midnight below us.
With each noon
a little ice age passes,

a glacier flows through
our cool chest. It melts
away under the blazing

headlines. History:
when I enter
its waters I step into

a time machine; all
our lives are back down there,
we wade out over

the shoals, lose ourselves
among small kin that nuzzle
our flesh and the bigger

jaws that let us pass. This
is memory, the balance
of salt against salt,

one drop and the Pacific.
Towards dawn muffled footsteps overhead
carry the horizon

on in our sleep,
the new day pours
its blue into our heads.

## VIII

We find our own way
back. Though all the signs
have fallen, the doors
we walked through out of childhood, leaving

houses empty shells bleached in the grass,
stand open. We close
our eyes and do not recognize the view.
Only the air

persists, a familiar touch, and an odour
we thought was of the leaves
is there, though the trees
are not. It is a quality of the isle;

another shore
is what this always was, we are at home there,
it is our body
we move through, reading

its strange geography
as Landscape (I), as Weather
(II), as Scenes from Childhood without number. Nothing
passes. Only Time

that ocean we step into
once, twice, as many
times as we dare lauch into its depths.
Back down there

we go on into
a new light not looking
ourselves, and neither forward now
nor back.

## READING A VIEW

Light soars twelve thousand feet into perfect blue. Fires are lit,
smoke disperses
between one line of hills, one fold
of cypress and the next, the next — the eye
moves deeper. Everything
in this view has occurred
before and is repeated leaf on leaf; all's aligned
in the one direction: a spade handle, rain
in broken verticals, a stand of pine that will be next year's
firewood; even our bodies
when we lay them out together
a distance from the earth. Reading a view
is seeing where each thing points to, irrespective
of the plane it's in, the arc on which it enters. What
does a sparrow in a hawk's foot
weigh against rocks
in their slow flight, the air
all dust and shelves of light,
arena of the day's real happenings?
We trace a lower path at the garden's edge, tending whatever
flaps, wads, spirals, hurls up sparks. The landscape
burns to be replaced. We are moving into
autumn, we say, or somewhere in that direction.
A leaf would show us where.

# THE LADDERS

This morning a truck is parked under my window; it is loaded with new ladders. Three, five, seven metres long, they will be used for olive picking. Oil is the life of this village, no meal eaten without it; but none of the local wood is tough enough for ladders. They are cut from chestnut poles, and brought down from the mountains whose snows next month will hang above us as we pick. Today the peaks are in cloud, we barely see them; and the olives are still green.

Peasants appear. They shift about and smoke, they consider the ladders, testing them for spring, for weight, for balance, counting the rungs; imagining how they will go up into the grey light of the olives, on uneven ground in wind.

It is still today. But the peasants have already moved into November; they walk as in heavy wind, swaying metres above the earth.

The man selling the ladders pushes his cap back and shrugs; his workmanship is good. The villagers count out notes, rung after rung, and walk away each with a ladder over his shoulder, one end firm in the crook of his arm, the other swaying. Unsteady as in wind.

I consider buying one. I would like to set my foot down on the bottom rung and climb; setting the ladder's foot in the street and climbing slowly hand over hand into next month's snow. Between here and the mountains there is commerce.

Night comes on. In the shed where the truck is parked, oil-stains run with rainbow colours. The ladders are horizontal, stacked in rows across the tray. I choose one and it rises.

High in the grey-green light something is ripening. Like a boy on stilts the ladder talks with clouds. Its shadow lies like a track across my sleep.

# THE SWITCH

I am looking for the switch in a darkened room. My hand travels the wall, touches this place and that of the dark surface. Nothing occurs. I hear a cricket's tap tap tap and wonder if that's the place, but can't locate it. The room seems bigger. Do rooms expand as they grow darker? I've never been in this room before, not this one. Everything I touch, even the things I placed here, are unfamiliar. The walls creak as if we were far out in the landscape, sailing low over the fields. The walls fall still as if we had arrived somewhere; so long ago that the forest has grown up round us. Beetles have drilled through the roof to let in starlight. The floor planks have softened, on their way to being the earth-floor of a forest. Is the current still connected? My hand moves over the walls. What am I looking for? A woodknot that when touched will slide the trees away, open my eyes to the horizon? I lie down in the dark among the shufflings, the flutterings. One of these sounds, if tracked to its source, would be my heart. What are the others? I settle for the dark. I lower myself into it and drift. It enters my ears, passes in and out of my mouth so I barely notice, touches my skin, touches the secret place on my surface that is the switch. Suddenly all the tracks that lead to this room are clearly visible, shining with footsteps. There are fingerprints, also visible, all over the walls.

# CARPENTER'S SHED

The place is cavernous. When you step in out of sunlight at whatever hour, in whatever season, it is half-dark and silent, a forest clearing laid on its side where all the timber is horizontal. Light filters through the rafters. It falls in solid shafts, another forest set at an angle to the first through whose ghostly trunks, as they flow upward, we see the granules of its breath.

Doorframes stand on chocks. They are always empty. Step through and you find yourself in another forest. There are windows. They have no view. Consult them at any hour and nothing enters: no coloured feather, no leaf, when night arrives no winking planets. Open one and you are high up on a sill on the seventh floor back in the forest. You call. Nobody hears.

Doors, windows, skirting-boards for rooms that exist as yet only in plan, though events are pressing. A suburb is visible now that the leaves are stripped, the trunks sawn into planks and the smaller limbs reduced to woodchip.

You come demanding something. I came for bookshelves; there are windows, there are coffins. The forest cracks its joints and moves away over the skyline; knowing, however far it's been transported, that the same piece goes on through the walls of houses, through bookshelves, dining tables, and the smooth planks of coffins, into the earth.

## THE CRAB FEAST

I

There is no getting closer
than this. My tongue slips into
the furthest, sweetest corner
of you. I know all

now all your secrets.
When the shell
cracked there was nothing
between us. I taste moonlight

transformed into flesh
and the gas bubbles rising
off sewage. I go down
under mangrove roots and berries, under the moon's

ashes; it is cool
down there. I always knew that there was more
to the Bay than its glitters,
knew if you existed

I could also
enter it; I'd caught so deeply all
your habits, knowing the ways
we differ I'd come to think we must be one.

I took you
to me. Prepared
a new habitat under the coral
reef of my ribs. You hang there, broken like the sun.

II

Noon that blinding glass did not reveal us
as we were. It cast up variant selves
more real than
reflections, forms

with a life of their own,
stalk eye a periscope
that determined horizons, Doulton claws
that could snap off a thumb.

I liked that. Hence the deep afternoons
with pole and net, the deeper
nights when I went down after the tropic
sun. Hence too the Latin

names, a dangerous clawhold. I wanted the whole of you, raw poundage
in defiance of breathlessness
or the power of verbal charms,
on my palm, on my tongue


III

This the Place. I come back
nightly to find it
— still, sleepy, sunlit, presided over

by old-timers, waterbirds whose one
thin leg props up clouds,
the ruck of open water

ahead, and the hours
of deepening blue on blue the land wades into after noon.
These then the perspectives:

matchwood pier, a brackish estuary
that flows on into
the sun, a rip of light over the dunes.

I enter. It is all
around me, the wash
of air, clear-spirit country. It goes on

all day like this. The tide
hovers and withdraws. Under the sun, under the moon's
cross-currents, shadows

fall into place
and are gathered to the dark. This hunt
is ritual, all the parties to it lost. Even the breaths

we draw between cries
are fixed terms in what is celebrated,
the spaces in a net.

Among mangrove trunks the fire
-flies like small hot love-crazed
planets switch on,

switch off. They too
have caught something. A chunk of solid midnight
thrashes in the star-knots of their mesh.


IV

You scared me with your stillness and I scared
myself. Knowing
that everything, even the footsoles of the dead, where your small
    mouths
nudged them, would feed

the airy process of it.
The back of my head
was open to the dream
dark your body moves in. I hunted you

like a favourite colour,
indigo, to learn
how changeable we are, what rainbows
we harbour with us

and how I should die, cast wheezing into
a cauldron of fog.
That was the plan:
to push on through

the spectrum to that perfect
primary death colour, out
into silence and a landscape
of endings, with the brute sky pumping red.


V

I watch at a distance
of centuries, in the morning
light of another planet
or the earliest gloom

of this one, your backward
submarine retreat,
as hoovering across
the seabed — courtly,

elate, iron-plated —
you practice the Dance.
I watch and am shut out.
The terrible privacies!

You move slow motion sideways,
an unsteady astronaut:
step and counter
step, then the clash,

soundless, of tank engagement;
you might be angels
in the only condition
our senses reach them in. I observe

your weightless, clumsy-tender
release. I observe
the rules; cut off
here in the dimension

of pure humanity, my need for air
a limiting factor,
I look through into
your life. Its mysteries

disarm me. Turning
away a second time
to earth, to air, I leave you
to your slow-fangled order,

taking with me
more than I came for
and less. You move back into
my head. No, it does not finish here.

VI

We were horizons
of each other's consciousness. All transactions
at this distance are small,
blurred, uninsistent. Drawn

by unlikeness, I grew
like you, or dreamed I did, sharing your cautious
sideways grip on things, not to be broken,
your smokiness of blood, as kin

to dragons we guarded
in the gloom of mangrove trunks
our hoard. I crossed the limits
into alien territory. One of us

will die of this, I told myself; and one of us
did. The other
swam off to lick warm stones and sulk with clouds along a shoreline;
regretting the deep

shelves and downward spaces,
breathing easy,
but knowing something more
was owed and would take place. I go down

in the dark to that encounter, the sun
at my back. On the sea-bed
your eyes on their sticks
click white in the flattened shadow of my head.


VII

A dreamy phosphorescence
paddles towards me. The moon drowses,
feeds, its belly white, its tough shell
black. We are afloat

together. You are
my counterweight there, I hang above you
in sunlight and a balance
is struck  No, the end

will not be like this.
We belong to different orders, and are trapped
by what we chose. Our kinship
is metaphorical, but no less deadly for all that,

old Dreadnought; as if I wore
black and carried death clenched in my fist. I do
wear black. My hand is open. It is my teeth
that seek you in the dark. And I approach bearing a death.


VIII

It was always like this: you
broken before me,
beautiful in all
the order of your parts, an anatomy lesson,

the simple continent
our bodies broke away from.
Because you are so open, because
the whole of your life

is laid out here, a chamber
to be entered and stripped. You have nothing
to hide. That sort of power
kills us, for whom

moonlight, the concept blue,
is intolerably complex as
our cells are, each an open universe
expanding beyond us, the tug

of immortality.
We shall reach it and still die.
I will be
broken after you, that was the bargain,

all this
a compact between us, who love
our privacies. I play
my part. Bent over you I dip my hand

in the bowl, I shake my cuffs, out in the open
and lost. Deep down
I am with you in the dark. The secret flesh of
my tongue enters a claw.

Because you are so open. Because you are.


IX

It is your weight
that hangs upon me. How
to deal with it. Hooded, claws locked
to your body like a star

you drag me under
the light of this occasion
to others. I've dreamed you once
too often. So this

is what it is to drown, this suffocating
torpor, giving up to
the drug of, the drag of
the moon. Here in your kingdom

I feel night harden over
my skull. That we should have come
so far out of the dark
together. I try to drown

well, I hold my breath,
no thrashing. Blue, majestic,
you blaze in my thoughts. Displacing more
than your real weight, making less

than the usual disturbance,
you plunge and take me with you.
I go out
in silence, in full view

of waiters; having learned
this much at least; to die true
to my kind — upright, smiling —
and like you, beyond speech.


X

No I am not ashamed
of our likeness, of what is in it that betrays me,
a smell of salt

backwaters, a native
grasp on the gist
of things, our local patch

of not-quite-solid earth from which the vast swing of the sky
is trackable. Night
comes on and I am caught

with a whole life on my hands,
in my mouth raw words,
the taste of so much air, so much water,

flesh. It was never to be weighed,
this dull shore and its landscape, water
poised above water

and all its swarming creatures, against the kingdom of cloud castles
we build with our breath.
But words made you

a fact in my head. You were
myself in another species, brute
blue, a bolt of lightning, maybe God.

Now all has been made plain
between us, the weights are equal, though the sky
tilts, and the sun

with a splash I do not hear breaks into
the dark. We are one at last. Assembled here
out of earth, water, air

to a love feast. You lie open
before me. I am ready.
Begin.

## FIRST THINGS LAST

I

The room on all sides viewless.
As if breathed on
glass, your cries
appear, ice crystals click.
A dense fog seeps in.
These are the fittings
of a clean, fluorescent, flat, unhappy country.

Its walls are soft. They melt
through you. Lift an arm
and weightless it drifts off. Other
parts of your body
are off elsewhere. You walk out over
(Careful, don't cut yourself —
that dream is red) soft breakers tipped with glass.

Only the instruments
are keen with a view
to business. They are unpacked
from a black bag, animal; the hands that use them
are also animal, and interested. Hot for blood
they start over the dazzling
absolute ice towards you, bringing night.


II

Behind you in the glass
a slow hand effaces
the room, wipes out
lake mist and forest.
Your smile

fades over the sill.
When the mirror
clears, no one stands
in the wet field that peals from
its surface. You stare

and stare. It takes days
of accounting for each hair
on your head, each grain of dust,
to imagine yourself
back into the frame.

You argue with the sky
in your mouth; you breathe out
clouds, get them moving
behind you, they lift
the grass, a little nightwind

arrives at your skin.
Slowly you manage
your head into the room. If you
can glue a face back on it,
you win.


III

We've all been in there: how
we got out, what passed, how long
we stayed is a black hole

or many in the fabric,
amnesias and pits we tumble into, deep
as first breath or the long drop where we missed

a step that was not there. Whole stars are swallowed
at a gulp. They shine
as velvet intermissions,

holes with a history. Those who come back
don't know that they have been there and have nothing
to tell. Such open

occasions in the net
are the shadow of spilt milk, black, that spirals upward, the angel's
preliminary sneeze sucked inside out.


IV

Laying the small bones out
in rows for the moon
to suck. We call this *Living
from One Day to the Next.*

To lie tight-wrapped in butcher's
paper and bleed
events: you all know this one:
it's *Learning from History.*

You mount a bicycle
without wheels. What falls away
as you pedal uphill?
*The Joys of the Flesh*

The styles are as many as
the players. Strict rules
apply but can be broken.
Nobody wins.

# ODE ONE

*For Sibylle and Vivian Smith*

The new day finds us here. We have come down
from the high lands of sleep in the company
of dreams, shy beasts whose scent is still upon us;
invisibly we herd them, feel the heat of
their breath. We are at home. The same sky stretches
on past yesterday. Orion fades
as blue beats up, tonight's hot stars already
there, burning in time continuous,
light or dark, on this shore or that other,
familiar, flat, our bodies will arrive at
with dawn — the body's self, a known country,
but caught in a foreign light, the promised weather

change even the saddest of old masters
tacitly predict, a patch of blue
in midnight canvases, a landscape touched
with such surprises as at twilight send
angels over the fields, though we interpret
their light as circus wagons, take their silence
for bells. We turn aside from miracles
to the plain facts of a case, having put ourselves
in service to *this* and *that*, the denominative
clowns who are double agents in an affair
more actual-fabulous of *is* and *were*.
Fabulous! All our natural history told

in spells, in brilliant transformation scenes,
as finger, choosing secession, walks away
as stag, a lung flares up as laurel bush,
an eye winks and is bird. Out of the dark
we bring these fictions forth to explain ourselves
before bicycles and clocks. The dynasties
are marked out on our palm, heroes enter
as a minor itch, and island cities melt
on the tongue. The body's syntax is baroque:
it elaborates, zigzags, detours, jumps the tracks;
which is to say, that where we are is always
where we meant to get to, the time being

ripe, the place sufficient, a mild terrain
with a climate, like all gardens, propitious for
the full life of each fruit, its blossom, rind
and fall. The coast is clear, though just off-shore
brute creatures roll and thunder, at night come in
-to view from cliffs we climb to out of sleep.
The sea, under a red star, boils the colour
of blood, but will be blue again (the colour
of blood) towards dawn. There are walks whose statues,
as the year declines, grow softer in our arms,
and forests where the mind meets all those shapes
it longs for, subjects drawn from geometry

who sing of perfect number, the language, abstract,
exact, of miracle, which on occasions
we hear as human speech. Though the body's ear
is deaf to it, some other part, the tongue,
a hair, is tuned to catch (tiny receiver
of another harmony) its messages:
the text of tomorrow's accident, the face
of one who steps from the traffic to become,
transfigured as in dreams, the one, the One.
It is all there in the music our bodies are
the score of, and will take place there. Skies already
cover the event, the healing sun

that lights it is the same we do not see
but follow when we turn away in sleep.
The play is continuous. Green jumps out
of leaves into a distance where our head
is dark but knows the colours of the night
rainbow just the same that arches over
our bed, and the creatures too are within reach.
Our bodies meet in another kind of order
than stroking knows or claws. Change is the dress
we wear before the gods. How else should they
perceive us as we are? who look smilingly
on fingernail and city, rose, hawk, eyelid — *opera.*

# A POOR MAN'S GUIDE TO SOUTHERN TUSCANY

*For Carlo Olivieri*

There are many voyages to be made in this room. It is an air-balloon, a yacht, an island among other islands, hot on occasion as Sumatra, when it sails in among the archipelagoes, at other times as chill white as a submarine in one of the passages under the ice-cap, with the sky grinding solid overhead.

There are also the voyages that are made *out of* the room, taking any one of its various exits; and I don't mean the door, which opens only into another room, and then another, and for that reason seems a tedious way out — we cross too much that is familiar before we come to our first surprise; nor even the two windows, one of which looks into a little paved garden with flowers in tubs and the other into a street where cats flatten themselves on the sunlit cobbles and old ladies sit knitting in cane-bottomed chairs; since to arrive at either of those pleasant enough destinations you would have to survive the drop; the first thirty feet might be the most interesting part of any journey in that direction. No, there are other lines of departure. I have pioneered several of them, marking points, making notes in my head, roughing out a map. If I now embark on a description of one or two of them, it is not to suggest that you take these particular journeys yourself (though you are welcome to, of course; I claim no monopoly) but to project for you some of the many possibilities. Getting out of the room is, in the end, your own affair. It's every man for himself.

Let us begin with the print, 145.5 x 113 cm, of Le Douanier Rousseau's *Joyeux Farceurs*, which occupies the west wall between the bookshelves and the door.

The recommended exit here — there may be others that lead to more interesting places, but this is the one I know and have explored a little — is between two long yellowish leaves, the fifth and the sixth, on the left hand side of the painting; you push them apart and go straight on through.

I suppose what I had expected to find, leaving the flat jungle of the picture's surface, which is lit neither by sun nor moon but exists as it were before the notion of light entered the visible world, was more green of the same variety, or something denser perhaps, great swags of foliage falling from a blue hole in the sky — vines, night-flowering orchids, round leaves covered with hair-like fibres that sting; the whole upheld by the smooth trunks of trees that themselves have no visible foliage but support, along with rows of flying-foxes folded asleep on their wings, the vast parasitic weight of it, glossy, dark, impregnated with the odour of rotting vegetation and the droppings of bats. A rainforest. That is what I expected, because I had it already in mind, and the surface of the painting seemed to invite the eye into further reaches of what it already presented, the depths of itself. But the surface, it seems, is simply surface. Paint. Not the beginnings, in one dimension, of what will further on become three-dimensional, but something like the curtain in a theatre, which may be painted with a Neopolitan bayscape or a stack of crystalline hills, all very cool and orderly, or a scene from the life of Orpheus and Eurydice; when the curtain finally goes up, we don't expect to find ourselves in a real or even a fictive Naples, nor do we expect the stage to reveal further dimensions of those classical hills — a world, I mean, of which the curtain was a flat section. The painted view rolls up into the dark and we find ourselves in the midst of something else again: family squabbles, public disorder, the bloodied beards and hacked stumps, the smoky dishes, the fogbound watchtowers and barbed-wire enclosures of another order of existence, and the cries that proceed from the open mouths, even if they happen to scan, are not at all classical in the sense that painted view was, nor cool. The shift from the second to the fourth dimension (is it?) has been made with no evidence of a middle ground, no suggestion of a continuous reality between the one and the other. We must provide that for ourselves; out of that moment of darkness between the jerking up of the curtain and where we suddenly find ourselves. It is like parting those leaves, with the sweat of creation on our hands that is all over everything in the Rousseau landscape, to discover a thunderous plain of ice, a lesson in life rather than art, which is, I suppose, just what it should be. The sky smokes, the sea smokes and swirls, bluish white; great solid clouds, ice-floes, grind against our brow. The air, as it rolls over us, is shaggy with breath. Polar bear. The animal heat of the bear's body is creating all that fog and melting the waste of ice in there. Its blood — hot, heavy — would turn all the sea's blue to its own colour in a great bleeding forth, a gushing that would fill the horizon of the viewer's skull. It is the heat of the monkeys' blood (or whatever those creatures are who huddle at the centre of Rousseau's jungle), or their passionate clasping, that the bear is in communion with. That is the channel that leads from the surface of the painting to where we now stand surrounded with ice; that is the corridor we have stumbled along, a single channel of blood, of heat, that runs from the monkey's heart to the bear's, from that tropical jungle whose leaves we parted to this plain on which the polar bear breathes out solid icebergs.

So then — a good day's march across a shifting terrain into the light of a polar sunset; which is also, when we look about, make a close survey of our surroundings, and jog our memory a little, another painting, of an earlier date than the Rousseau, expressive, we might want to say, of another stage of culture and a different national consciousness — as well, of course, as another mind: it is *The Sea of Ice* of Kaspar David Friedrich. We have walked across out of one painting into another; passed several decades and a border-post or two, where the customs official (bearded) paid no attention to our "Nothing to declare" and rummaged about in our bags for gold, feathers, and found nothing — not even that upturned milk bottle that has somehow got into the Rousseau jun jungle and with its contents suspended there, frozen bluish white, might be the real connecting link. The bear has slipped away through a hole in the ice (like Kaspar David Friedrich's brother) or has simply melted into the landscape. These shattered ice-slabs are his bones. This fleecy grey-white sea, with its polar highlights, must be his pelt (or have we at last got into the bear's cranium, where the tide of blood flows blue?) — Well, enough for one brief excursion. This route obviously could be explored further, but I for one am happy to leave it there, to be returned to on a later occasion. This far or a mile further, what does it matter? There is only one final point to any journey, and for that we are not yet ready, are we? If we were, the quickest way out would have been via the window.

Let us swiftly turn back: across the smoky ice-plain, between the fronds, so! We are back in the room again and ready to start out now in a new direction.


There is, on the flat whitewashed wall of the room, about halfway up the frame of the window that looks into the street, and approximately five centimetres in the direction of the west wall, a stain or spot of mould in the shape of a wide-brimmed hat; you must imagine its being seen in profile and from slightly above.

If you look closely and long enough, this hat-shaped dark place on the wall, which would fit comfortably on your little fingernail, is also a place of exit, but one that leads, apparently, in different directions depending on whether you see the hat as lying on white sand (having blown from the head of a passing rider, whose hoofprints would also be visible on the wall if the wind hadn't drawn a fine layer of sandgrains over them [here we enter a desert of considerable dimensions, but with the hope at least of clear blue skies and an oasis or two — what travellers we might join there, with what elaborate tales to tell after the manner of such places, like the layers of an onion whose fumes already reach our nostrils, and O how the tears start for the fate of all those lost travellers in each of those tales in each layer of the onion!]); or is lying, that hat, on the clean white topsheet of a bed, having been tossed there by some careless hand that forces thereby, since the hat tossed on the bed is a fatal gesture, a momentary bend in the course of things that will lead inevitably to a death (But whose? That is what we want to know, and right now; it's no good saying Later, or We'll tell you when the time is ripe or when we get there. Now, we say. Now!); or the hat may not be a real hat at all but the shadow of a hat thrown against the wall by a light striking past the hat itself, etc., as physics will explain; in which case the hat itself must be very far off indeed, since the shadow is so much smaller than any real hat could be, and considering the laws of physics, etc., must lie beyond the furthest wall of the room; in which case we have problems for which physics offers no aid. One wonders where, out there, the real hat might be; where the source of light is that is casting the shadow; in which direction the head is turned that might be discovered under the hat (would that help?), since the head, like the hat, must be in some place further than the opposite wall, and what lies beyond that wall, we already know, is the kitchen.

But I think the possibilities afforded by this particular exit are already clear. Clear enough anyway for a jaunt on a summer afternoon, in company or alone with the labrador, whistling a nice tune ("La Follia d'Espagna" is a nice tune and will take you a long way), or turning over silently in your head as you trudge up the first sand dune or sit, hands clasped between your knees, on the narrow bed, with the hat safely on a wall peg at last — turning over silently in your head, I say, which will be hatless, the few clouds you have brought along with you which will pass on into clear weather or blow up later into a storm with lightning effects in saffron pink ... Anyway, you will have got the Idea by now and can make your own way. These are suggestions, not fully organized package tours, and are meant to provide for the traveller's own initiative. (But the hat may also, I'd suggest, be falling slowly through a white sky, with or without a head under it. In that case the journey may be a very short one, and as we know from a previous page there is a quicker route in that direction via the window.) Well, I leave things, at this point, hanging. Over to you.


The room contains a good sound-system: let us be rash and say "the best that money can buy". The listener, the traveller on air, lying flat on the cool woven-straw matting (which smells of Asia), or reclining in one of the two leather chairs (which smell of giraffe), having placed himself at the apex of the two converging lines from the speakers, with earphones if he wishes, or without if he prefers his music impure, overlaid, that is, with the random noises of the world — a fly droning at the window pane and unable to get out into that particular section of sky, the clank of sheepbells, the *creak creak* of crows as they flap behind a harvester, the buzz of a 99cc "motorino" as it climbs uphill under the pines, the ritual exchanges of a children's game, the boom of a jet laying down on the silence a trail of purest light, the almost inaudible rasping of dust grains as they sift down the walls, the hissing of thread out of the spider's mouth, the turbulence of particles of air as they bounce off irregular surfaces, wood, cloth, paper — with the earphones, then, in the silence of your own head and its distant beat of blood, or without, among the multiple sound layers of an August afternoon, the listener may hear .... But the choice is his, not mine; is yours, I mean. There are three shelves of records, a stock of silences that can at any moment be entered on the point of a needle and broken to yield hours of unbroken sound. What I would myself recommend, since I have found it more than sufficient on occasion, is Donizetti's *Lucia di Lammermoor*; to be precise, the Joan Sutherland second version, the Mad Scene, and a note at the very end, a high E-flat, that is an exit of quite extraordinary promise, a lovely wide velvet-lined corridor that we oughtn't to think of as proceeding from (or in this case leading back to) the throat of a particular soprano, or as being in any way a fixed station (however much it may resemble certain old-fashioned stage perspectives) on the line of Lucia's flight from reality, her madness, but as being rather an absolute avenue down which we move at incredible speed and where the air that fills our bloodstream brings with it the first clear certainty of an impending lightness, the possibility of flight. We are breathing, for as long as the note lasts, eternal E-flat weather, the atmosphere of another planet, whose note, as the planet spins, is always this one; so that we have to be grateful to Donizetti, to Lucia, to Sutherland, for so gracefully, so swiftly transporting us there, since it is not given to all of us to leap thus from planet to planet and that particular sphere is out of reach of all but the rarest of us — though to be able to reach it at all is, when one of our species makes the miraculous scoop and lands there, an achievement that brings glory to us all, even if we can only come to it, rather clumsily, via the ear, while our breath goes on being the air of our home planet, earth, this stretch of it, this August, this room.

It's a great way out. One, as you will appreciate, of so many that the mere possibility of all those journeys stacked on the shelves quite takes our breath away. How could we ever, in one lifetime, take even a hundredth of them? It offers one a vision of eternity, measured out as it were in operas, and a hope of immortality, since the sounds surely wouldn't have come into existence if we were not to have the opportunity of exploring them — and a glimpse also of infinite space, in which every note struck is another planet to be yearned for, since the high E-flat in *Lucia* breathes quite a different atmosphere from the same note, *Es in alt*, in the first aria of the Queen of the Night.

But it is enough surely, it is enough. *Du holde Kunst*, a dear one sings, *ich danke dir dafür*, then turns away and draws breath out of the silence. Thanks indeed.

## AN DIE MUSIK

We might have known it always: music
is the landscape we move through in our dreams, and in the Garden
it was music we shared
with the beasts. Even plants
unbend, are enchanted. A voice wading
*adagio* through air, high, clear, wordless, opens perspectives
in the deepest silence; clovers
hum; the jungle's layered
sound-mix seeks horizons, arranging itself as avenues.

What else does it make,
this *concert champetre*, if a not a space we might re-enter
in innocence, pure steps
of sound on which the creatures
descend at almost dusk to recognize, as in a pool,
their names (not *cat*, not *Moggy*), and passion-flowers
incline their busy flywheels to the sun, spinning a line
of melody that modulates from yellow
to green as in mirror fugues and counter-clockwise through the year.

So then, play your beanfield
Vivaldi's *Gloria* and see the thin pods swell, miraculous and many
as the mouths of Hosannah. Watch them
explode across a stave, the angel syllables,
zip-fresh, sky-packed, and flutter
*prestissimi* on strings in hemidemisemiquavers.
Let the countryside be filled
with a din, a chime, an agricultural boom, real orchestras
(the Boston Pops) in real market gardens.

Imagine as *Ein Heldenleben* blooms
in a paddock, the slow inner lives of pumpkins, big stones
cracking, a moon-washed field
astir like a symphony as Bruckner coaxes the zucchini.

The green things of the earth
discover a fifth season to push through to, all
grace notes, as their vegetable souls
aspire to "the condition". A new species
taps at the boundaries. Beethoven's Tenth is what it breathes.

## ODE:

Schubert, Sonata in B Flat Major, D.960 (op. posth.)

But this was not predicted: none of the angels
— notebook, night hawk, girl at the box-office —
foretold this autumn landscape, the clear gift
shines through all its wrappings, unwraps itself
of haze and is distributed as stubble
and small stones take the sun. Walls dissolve
and the starched clouds roll back with no applause
to mark a change of scene. All this was ours
from the start. In our desert cave the river, shifting
underground, moved on and here re-enters
our lives, out of the broken light of mirrors
unwinds its images. They approach

with the odd look of friends that we have failed
to greet across a square, a lion our eye
mistook for Whitsun roses, or that day
in K.L. when a dream of windmills battered
all morning in my head and blew up such
a storm among our papers — but you remember
as I do how it was. And now such bland
reflections ripple in as evening arrives
from towns back in the hills where terraced gardens
nod over a bluff; having passed so many
seasons on the way and seen such gathering
of leaves, armies, voices. Tomorrow remains

unspoken in the boughs, an accumulation
of light in deep allees where footprints lead us
on into ourselves, and the reluctant
stone that was these hills discovers the limbs
of tall gods locked within, requiring only
breath, faith — our faith — and the sculptor's hand
to wake and walk among us. Pointing off
to cliffs from which they came, untouched by time
in their stillness and perfection, they pine for softness,
to reach out and touch, to be touched at last
by change; they envy the candied ray that fades
on petals, and the rainbow that dries up

in linen after the tear-storms of bereavement.
And so to have arrived today among
these pure occasional wonders is both surprise
and no surprise at all. The ordinary
facts transmuted here are what we knew
from the outset but had not seen from just this angle
of late days, where grains of dust sift through
the bowl of air as through an hourglass, turning
our faces to the night of mountainous cloud
on cloud. These recoveries, as of a motif
scattered and reformed out of itself,
are the old life re-invented. A door flies open

in the new house and the same paddock dazzles
our eyes, the still earth murmurs with its many
mouths, oracular springs, fresh waters running
away through cleft and channel to odd places
of exile, or the sea whose larger music
they enter as a sigh — their exit thunder
on a far beach at dawn. It takes a lifetime
to gather that life is full of such reprises
and echoes, raindrops flinging a river's light
in fragments on the pane. No longer to be
singular, absorbed in a solemn cloud
of knowing too much to enter the charmed circle

of things, that is the key. Take heart, we say.
Take heart, take all, and make of it what you will.
It will always be the same flood pounding
through you, the same arc that bends beyond
the imaginably familiar. That is how
it is with us. These topiary beasts are figures
in a strict geometry; new leaves enter
the scene, start for a point of clipped perfection
they'll never reach, who belong always to nature
and fall. But green returns, that is the point.
These fallings are part of it; a clue of gold
unravels through these aimless days of autumn,

spilled grass, leaf wrack, the scene remains itself,
holding its colours back a while before
it turns and shakes them loose. Though we stand staring
at blank mirrors sheeted with our prayers,
the pollens glow, the avenues lead out
from here; we have only to catch our breath, reversing
the image, reversing time, to walk back into
the room with its open door and the earth unwrapping
gifts out of the mist. Wet furrows shine.
On slopes among hedge and cypress the sentinel
statues lift their brows into cloud country.
We could live for ever here. We could live for ever.

## ODE: STRAVINSKY'S GRAVE

Transposing our bodies
in grey light to the island
graveyard, we
were aware (as many

who make this water journey
are not) that intervals
of stillness and silence
are music between times

solid enough,
among mist and the marsh bird's
calling, to sustain
a man's weight, a cathedral's

centuries of shifting
from the right knee to the left.
The Campanile
ticks, a metronome

conducting the wavelets
on past lines-of-washing
tenements that hang
on a breath. The dead keep

an ear to the ground,
have time to grow accustomed
to the beat. Our senses
cannot support

such whiteness as the dome
of heaven breathes into
existence. Music gives it
colour and key,

it flows and is blue
if the day is, black,
or at night a piano-roll
punched with light and tumbling

sonatas. We stay among the dead,
observing how the twentieth century
favours the odd
conjunction and has made

strange bedfellows. (Not all of us
would rejoice at the last trump
to discover we'd been laid
by Diaghilev). The parting

bell tolls over us,
and those who can, and we
among them, re-embark.
The weather's shifted

ground so many times
in minutes, it might be
magic or miracle and you the day's
composer as you are

the century's, though at home among
immortals. We go back
the long way via the dead
silence of the Arsenal, its boom

raised, its big guns open
-mouthed before the town.
I talk to a Negro kid
from New Jersey, thinking of what

my travellers cheques will buy
(which also work
by numbers) whoever stole them
from me — not Fame, not Love; and how

we put out crumbs to catch
birds and such scraps
of sky as are filled with
a singing; and what like Love

is not to be caught
by intent, the longer breath
of late works. A city
wades out of the dark

towards us. Our boat
falls still, steadies a moment,
then rides
in among the watery monuments.